Year 4

Handwriting
Activity Workbook

Parrot

Home learning from the experts

Author:
Sarah Loader

About this book

This book supports the practice and consolidation of handwriting skills, with lots of engaging, fun activities to help children grow in confidence and ability.

Clear, consistent, cursive handwriting is not only a statutory requirement of the English curriculum, but is the gateway to success in all subjects. The ability to present ideas legibly and clearly is a critical life skill.

Handwriting made clear

- Handwriting requires strong fine-motor skills and pencil control. The tasks in this activity book develop and refine those skills.
- Key skills are learned and reinforced through a wide range of tasks to keep children engaged and interested in each activity.
- Helpful tips and reminders support children as they work.

How to use this book

- Little-and-often is a productive approach to handwriting, as handwriting requires great concentration and can be frustrating. Children can work through just one or two activities in a sitting, and stop when they lose interest to avoid it becoming negative.
- Try to complete the activities in the given order, as they progress in challenge and expectation.
- Your child will ideally work through activities independently, but it's worth being there for when support is needed.
- Explore the Progress Points with your child as they work through the book to see where further support is needed.

Getting started

- Make your child's learning space interesting and fun.
- Encourage your child to step away from any technology or energetic games a little while beforehand, and to take some deep breaths to help them focus.
- Make sure your child is holding their pencil properly.
- Sit with your child to start with, even if you're occupied with your own task.

Challenges to overcome

Keeping handwriting neat and consistent
Maintaining consistent and neat handwriting is tricky. Children may need reminders throughout writing tasks, specifically about the height and length of letters.

Ensuring letters look the same each time they appear
The focus on handwriting looking the same across all their writing is important as children progress – so practising writing for different purposes is useful.

Get creative

- To enable longer handwriting practice, you could cut up a newspaper article into paragraphs and ask children to structure it and write it out.
- Children could try writing longer passages that still have some structure – for example, a book review, an alternative ending to a book, a character profile.
- You could provide children with a fictional or real headline (and sub-headings if they need more structure) and ask them to write an article to match the subject.

English curriculum coverage

As well as covering the Year 4 handwriting statutory requirements, this activity book develops and practises handwriting skills within the context of the wider English curriculum, so that tasks and activities are meaningful and relevant for children. Some of these objectives are taken from the previous year as useful revision.

Topic	Curriculum relevance
Homophones	English Appendix 1: Spelling (work for Years 3 and 4)
Suffixes	English Appendix 1: Spelling (work for Years 3 and 4)
Spellings ending –sure and –ture	English Appendix 1: Spelling (work for Years 3 and 4)
Contractions	English Appendix 1: Spelling (work for Year 2)
Headings and sub-headings	Writing – Composition (Years 3 and 4)
Fronted adverbials	Writing – Vocabulary, grammar and punctuation (Years 3 and 4)
Spellings ending –sion, -tion, -ssion, -cian	English Appendix 1: Spelling (work for Years 3 and 4)
Direct speech	Writing – Vocabulary, grammar and punctuation (Years 3 and 4)
Organising paragraphs around a theme	Writing – Composition (Years 3 and 4)
Prefixes	English Appendix 1: Spelling (work for Years 3 and 4)
Writing narratives	Writing – Composition (Years 3 and 4)

Activity 1

Write out the sentences, choosing the correct homophone to complete each one.

> Homophones are words that sound the same, but have different spellings and meanings.

ball / bawl   except / accept   break / brake   groan / grown

1. Remember to [?] if going downhill.

_____

2. No one can go in there [?] for teachers.

_____

3. If she falls over she will [?] her eyes out.

_____

4. In the dark I could hear a loud [?].

_____

5. Adam had [?] a lot since I'd last seen him.

_____

6. My favourite part of the school day is [?] time.

_____

7. Pat passed the [?] to me and I scored.

_____

8. Dad said I just had to [?] his decision.

_____

1 I can write homophones.

Activity 2

Write out each word adding the suffix 'ous'.
Remember to join together your letters.

danger   _____

mountain _____

poison   _____

courage   _____

outrage   _____

Activity 3

Write a sentence for each word in Activity 2.

1. _His voice took on a dangerous tone._ _____

2. _____

3. _____

4. _____

5. _____

Activity 4

Rewrite the sentences, choosing a word from the box to complete each one.

treasure   adventure   pleasure   furniture
nature   measure   picture

1. I look for hidden [?] at the seaside.

   _____

2. I'm always keen for a new [?].

   _____

3. Look at the [?] I did at Art Club!

   _____

4. Matt had to [?] his feet for new shoes.

   _____

5. Paul helped us to move the [?].

   _____

6. You can go for a [?] cruise around the bay.

   _____

7. Dixie loves being outdoors and enjoys [?].

   _____

2 I can write words with –ure spellings.

Activity 5

Write these contractions out as full words.

I'm	*I am*	we'll	_____
I'll	_____	we'd	_____
I've	_____	he's	_____
I'd	_____	she'll	_____

Activity 6

Write a sentence for each contraction from Activity 5.

1. *I'm nine years old.* _____

2. _____

3. _____

4. _____

5. _____

6. _____

7. _____

8. _____

Activity 7

Write out the facts about India, presenting each one under its correct heading.

Continent   Capital city
Population   Currency   Size   Major mountain range
Major river   Terrain   Religions
Native animals

- Asia
- New Delhi
- 1,236,344,631
- Rupee
- 3,287,590 square kilometres
- Himalaya
- Ganges
- Desert, jungle, plain, mountains
- Hindu, Muslim, Buddhism, Sikhism, Jainism
- Elephants, bears, snow leopards, pythons, rhinos, tigers, sharks, crocodiles, dolphins, turtles

All About India

India

Continent Asia	
Capital city	

Activity 8

Write out the sentences, choosing the correct homophone to complete each one.

effect / affect   fair / fare   reign / rain   heal / he'll

1. The goal was definitely not ? .

   _____

2. I don't think we should go out in this ? .

   _____

3. He says ? be home by six.

   _____

4. Ally still feels the ? of the storm.

   _____

Activity 9

Write a sentence of your own for one homophone in each pair.

1. _____

2. _____

3. _____

4. _____

Activity 10

Rewrite each sentence with the underlined adverbial phrase placed at the beginning of the sentence as a fronted adverbial. Remember to start each sentence with a capital letter.

Don't forget! Always follow a fronted adverbial with a comma.

1. We're going on holiday <u>tomorrow</u>.

   <u>Tomorrow, we're going on holiday.</u>

2. We went to the park <u>yesterday</u>.

   _____

3. I was playing chase <u>at the park</u>.

   _____

4. We're going to school <u>after breakfast</u>.

   _____

5. I'm going away with Ted <u>next week</u>.

   _____

6. I'm singing in the choir concert <u>at school</u>.

   _____

Activity 11

Rewrite the sentences, choosing a word from the box to complete each one.

division   television   occasion   invasion
collision   decision

1. I love watching [?] after school.

   _____

2. My team is in the second [?].

   _____

3. Reading my diary is an [?] of my privacy.

   _____

4. Mum's made her final [?].

   _____

5. The [?] between the two cars was serious.

   _____

6. The party was a happy, fun [?].

   _____

3 I can write words with –sion spellings.

Activity 12

Write out the sentences, choosing the correct homophone to complete each one.

meddle / medal   mail / male   where / wear   main / mane

1. We're always told not to ? .

    _____

2. The opposite of female is ? .

    _____

3. The ? point was to write about the trip.

    _____

4. The queen has to ? a heavy crown.

    _____

Activity 13

Write a sentence of your own for one homophone in each pair.

1. _____

2. _____

3. _____

4. _____

4 I can write homophones.

Activity 14

> Write the correct contraction for each pair of words. Think about which letters to join together.

who is   <u>who's</u>   they are   _____

they have   _____   he will   _____

it is   _____   she is   _____

we are   _____   they will   _____

Activity 15

> Write a sentence for each contraction.

1. <u>Who's coming to my party?</u>

2. _____

3. _____

4. _____

5. _____

6. _____

7. _____

8. _____

5 I can write contractions.

Activity 16

Rewrite the sentences, choosing a word from the box to complete each one.

communication injection invention celebration
education hesitation eruption

1. The [?] didn't hurt at all.

_____

2. The wedding [?] went on all night.

_____

3. The volcano [?] was enormous.

_____

4. There was a [?] before Nara spoke.

_____

5. I think my [?] is more original.

_____

6. I need to improve my [?] skills.

_____

7. The standard of [?] is very high.

_____

6 I can write words with –tion spellings.

Activity 17

Write out each of the words from the box in the correct column, adding the suffix 'ly' or 'ous' to each one.

> sad   quiet   danger   poison   final
> courage   loud   outrage

Words with 'ly' suffix	Words with 'ous' suffix
_____	_____
_____	_____
_____	_____
_____	_____

Activity 18

Write two sentences of your own, one containing one of the 'ly' words, and one containing one of the 'ous' words.

_____

_____

_____

_____

Activity 19

Write out the text, adding speech marks in the correct places.

Remember to start each person's speech on a new line.

As the ball hit the back of the net, there was a roar around the stadium. I can't believe it, I said to Steph. I think we might actually win this. Don't speak too soon, Steph said, as the ball was run down towards the far goal. No, please no, I whispered. The striker took a shot. Then suddenly a cheer ripped through the crowd. He's hit the post, Steph shouted. They've done it! I said. Come on, let's get chips on the way home, Steph said.

_____

_____

_____

_____

_____

_____

_____

_____

_____

Activity 20

Rewrite the sentences, choosing a word from the box to complete each one.

expression   admission   permission   discussion
aggression   impression   confession

1. I need (?) to leave class.

   _____

2. My (?) of Elsie is that she's very shy.

   _____

3. The (?) price has gone up a lot.

   _____

4. Leo does taekwondo to get out his (?).

   _____

5. His (?) was one of utter delight.

   _____

6. After a long (?), Mum let me go.

   _____

7. I should make a (?) about the test.

   _____

7 I can write words with –ssion spellings.

Activity 21

Rewrite the sentences, choosing a word from the box to complete each one.

tremendous   hideous   glamorous   various
jealous   precious   momentous   ferocious

1. The beast had a [?] dirty face.

   _____

2. I was [?] of the guys picked for the team.

   _____

3. Being school captain was a [?] honour.

   _____

4. There are always [?] options for lunch.

   _____

5. Mum looks [?] when she goes out.

   _____

6. The first day at my new school was [?].

   _____

7. His huge, [?] jaws snapped shut.

   _____

8. This necklace is very [?] to me.

   _____

Activity 22

Write out this postcard, using the words in the box to complete it.

luckily   jealous   various   nervous
incredibly   courageous

Dear Mum and Dad, I'm having an unbelievable time here. We've done [?] water sports, like surfing and snorkelling. The snorkelling was [?] exciting, but I found the surfing made me a bit [?] at first. Abdul thinks I will feel more [?] next time, and [?] I can try it again tomorrow. I can't wait! I hope this postcard hasn't made you too [?]! Love from Ryan

_____

_____

_____

_____

_____

_____

_____

Activity 23

Rewrite the sentences, choosing a word from the box to complete each one.

> magician   optician   musician   electrician
> politician   paediatrician   technician

1. The [?] played the violin beautifully.

   _____

2. The tricks the [?] did were amazing!

   _____

3. An [?] came and fixed the lights.

   _____

4. A [?] is a children's doctor.

   _____

5. Kit went to the [?] for an eye test.

   _____

6. The [?] helps the community.

   _____

7. The [?] set up all the equipment.

   _____

8 I can write words with –cian spellings.

Activity 24

The text and headings in this leaflet have got mixed up. Rewrite the leaflet with each paragraph matched to the right heading. Remember to join your letters.

What Do You Know About Tigers?

Tigers are one of the largest big cats in the world – here's everything you need to know about them.

Where They Live

Tigers weigh up to 300 kg and have a unique striped pattern on their bodies.

What Their Future Looks Like

Tigers are carnivores, which means they eat meat, like deer, wild boar and rodents. Tigers hunt on their own and get close to their prey before they attack.

What They Look Like

Tigers live wild in lots of different environments – tropical forests, grasslands and mangrove swamps. They live in India, China, Russia and South-East Asia.

What They Eat

Tigers are endangered because their habitat is being destroyed and because they are killed. Today, only 3,900 tigers live in the wild.

<u>What Do You Know About Tigers?</u>
<u>Tigers are one of the largest big cats in the world –</u>
<u>here's everything you need to know about them.</u>

(9) I can write an organised text.

Activity 25

The titles and blurbs of these books have got mixed up. Draw a line to match them up correctly and then neatly write out each title and blurb together.

Sleepover at Jenny's

Sailing Across the Atlantic

The Beast of Monroe

The Haunted Wood

Anita had been looking forward to Jenny's sleepover for weeks. Finally the day had arrived – and she couldn't wait!

No one knows if it's real or fantasy, but the legend of the Beast of Monroe has been alive for centuries. One man sets out on an epic journey to find the truth.

Jack and his best friend Al hadn't believed the rumours about the wood being haunted... until now. Would they be able to escape unharmed?

As I set out on the greatest challenge of a lifetime, I had no idea what lay ahead of me, but it was too late to turn back.

Activity 26

> Read the opening of this story and predict what will happen next. Write the next two paragraphs in your best handwriting.

> I knew something was wrong the moment I stepped into the woods. It was still – too still – and an eerie silence hung in the air. I looked around and saw something hidden in amongst the trees…

⑩ I can write neatly on the line.

Activity 27

Write the correct word from the box next to each prefix.

happy graph appoint correct possible market
heading clockwise responsible behave turn national

dis _____   sub _____

mis _____   re _____

in _____   super _____

un _____   inter _____

im _____   anti _____

ir _____   auto _____

Activity 28

Choose four words to use in sentences
of your own.

1. _____

2. _____

3. _____

4. _____

Activity 29

Rewrite this newspaper article in your best handwriting, adding in a catchy headline and sub-headings to organise it into paragraphs.

It's been six weeks since the rubbish was last collected in Brinstown, due to the strike. Piles of bin bags fill the streets, particularly in the busy town centre where shops and restaurants are putting rubbish out every day. Because of the recent heatwave, food and waste are rotting and attracting rodents and insects. Talks are ongoing, but with no sign of a settlement. People are advised to keep rubbish to a minimum and to take their waste to a landfill site to reduce the impact on the streets.

II I can organise
text into paragraphs.

Activity 30

Rewrite this information about the Tour de France, presenting it as a fact file with different headings and features, such as 'Did You Know?' boxes for interesting facts.

The Tour de France is a men's bike race that is held every summer in France. The race is made up of 21 stages. Each stage is a day long and there are two rest days. The whole race is over 2,000 km. Each stage is timed and the rider with the fastest time wears the yellow jersey. The Tour de France is the largest sporting event in the world and over 12 million people stand along the route to cheer the cyclists on. The race has been going since 1903 and has only not run during the First and Second World Wars. Although the race starts and finishes in France, the route often visits nearby countries such as the Netherlands, Italy, Belgium, Germany, Luxembourg, Spain and Switzerland. During each stage of the race, the average cyclist will burn the same number of calories as there are in 252 double cheeseburgers!

12 I can use headings and features.

My name is _____